Hospital Series

Hospital Series

AMELIA ROSSELLI

Translated from the Italian by Deborah Woodard,
Roberta Antognini, and Giuseppe Leporace

NEW DIRECTIONS POETRY PAMPHLET #19

Serie ospedaliera was first published in 1969 by Il Saggiatore (Milan, Italy).

Grateful acknowledgment is made to the Centro di Ricerca sulla Tradizione Manoscritta di
Autori Moderni e Contemporanei at the University of Pavia for granting permission to publish
this edition. Publication was made in part possible by a grant from the Lucy Maynard Salmon
Research Fund. We are thankful to the Vassar College Research Committee for its support.

Some of these poems first appeared, often in a different version, in the following journals:
Action Yes, Artful Dodge, Chelsea, Common Knowledge, Kritya, Poetry Northwest, and *The Spoon
River Poetry Review.* A handful also appeared in *The Dragonfly: Selected Poems of Amelia Rosselli,
1953–1981* (Chelsea Editions, 2009)—special thanks to Alfredo de Palchi.

Cover design by Erik Carter
Interior design by Eileen Krywinski and Erik Rieselbach
Manufactured in the United States of America
New Directions Books are printed on acid-free paper.
First published as New Directions Poetry Pamphlet #19 in 2015

Library of Congress Cataloging-in-Publication Data
Rosselli, Amelia, 1930–1996.
[Poems. Selections English.]
Hospital series / Amelia Rosselli ; Translated from the Italian by Deborah Woodard, Roberta
Antognini, and Giuseppe Leporace.
pages cm
ISBN 978-0-8112-2397-3 (alk. paper)
I. Woodard, Deborah, translator. II. Antognini, Roberta, translator. III. Leporace, Giuseppe,
translator. IV. Rosselli, Amelia, 1930–1996. Hospital series. V. Rosselli, Amelia, 1930–1996.
Hospital series Italian. VI. Title.
PQ4878.O8A2 2015
851'.914—dc23   2014038438

10 9 8 7 6 5 4 3 2 1

ndbooks.com

New Directions Books are published for James Laughlin
by New Directions Publishing Corporation
80 Eighth Avenue, New York 10011

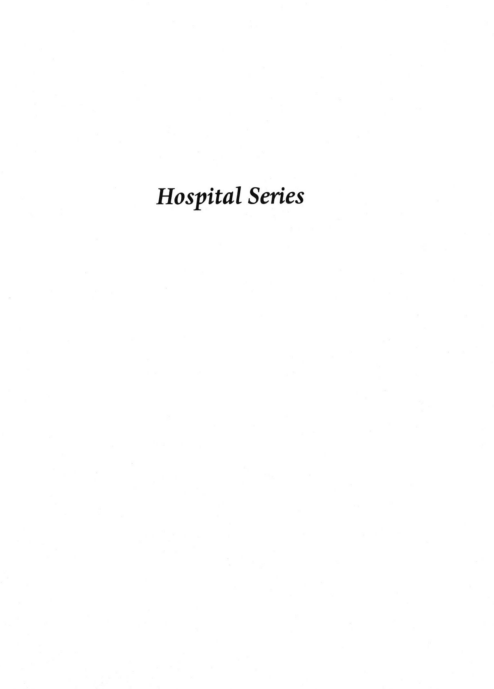

Hospital Series

By an experience impossible and dauntless
we laboriously ruptured isolation, but
the wagons that carried us like fruit to
market were gloomy automobiles white
if it snowed, infernal in the rain. Corrupting
guard upon guard the mind settles upon
a labored checkpoint for it deceived
even itself: the party was an encounter
of fashionable devils, each love fled
when you unlatched the window of your
poisoned power on the arm of my
enchantment poor attempt at envy, but
the spirit triumphed again with poor
decisions made in the cellar.

      After suffering and
hidden desperation Sunday was a
reprieve and a desperation, the sea in
motion muffled the spirit's quarrels while
gearshifts brought relief and the guilt
was guilt acknowledged if desperation
motions on toward bliss.

•

seventy beggars and a shirt tearing itself
in the naught, on a lark I stretched out in the
naught and all was laurel and beneficence, beneficiated
the king of the poor, slithering camel. A hard,
light rain penetrated, in need of assistance
I penetrated into rooms furnished for a truer life
which in capital letters slipped away from mine, most
obliging were those condemned to death. Invitations
slithered across the rain-drenched hinges of a permeable
city: no hidden beast powdered the goats
marching enraptured toward the mounts of the
Trinity: a camel, two Indians, and the people master
of all the arts, music and mathematics, the furor
of realizable dreams. Lost in the pool of shadows
white spider webs and powder for the eyelashes,
grains of sand and small pearls under a most miserable rain
wisely settled on a shuttered life.

•

Two monkeys furrowed the soul with invisible tracks, the
heart took it hard, old mustached sentinel, corrupt,
drunk, tenacious, without hope yet expecting the whole
curved sky on its sleeve. Does the heart have a sleeve? you ask and
irony it, too, besleeved (cookie-riddled)
draws or scratches a tremulous arabesque on the opaque hills
of the brain: irony's a needle, storms bathe with
opaque sadness the wanton blood, oh how breath runs

to cut off the sentinels! (here lunacy you pulled off a
kind of party, freed me.)

●

Harsh the three-way sentence. On the outs with the archipelago
we were swept away by the river, inorganic event, land and sea
spat blood instead. As you left, I saw myself in the vast
archipelago that was my mind so rigorous, logical,
desperate from such a void: one battle, two, three battles

lost. But the furor of our glances, you lantern
that thought to guide, I broken winch, but the furor
of these looks of ours foiled us: victory assured
the battle won the bandits stronger than us, the union
of two souls one tarantella.

●

The melancholy moon bent down tearful.

Innocent rivulets, half-empty boats, large lakes in the mountains
premise my being yours, and obedient.

•

Your watercolors discomposed my mind
loquacious from winterstice. Throughout spring's
discomfiture, I, storm-tossed ship, was still craftily
scaling the bright carousels: drowned treasure
yours and mine. The paintbrush quivered gently
in the simplicity of a shack discomposed by winter
that was an unremitting cruelty, a sleep of yours hidden
from my prayers, a slipping away from railroad tracks
often sliding toward my head instead, bowed
when there was light.

And the light discomposing into equal parts evolved
economical colors of the trainman's map.

Pale, exhausted, wrathful you warded off swallows
while I painted equally enamored of
nature and my need.

•

a sky-blue sun, a sprinkle of clotted crystal
early morning, the lights still on, neighborhoods teeming

with senility, the laundress with a basket but her shoulders
tremble. Small doses of ingrained tranquility! red the

indisposition, if your mind slumbers.

●

Sex violent as an object (quarry of whitened marble)
(curved amphora of clay) and artfully concealed in the form
of an egg assailed the solitary one, as though hail were
storming, in the living room. Not sybaritic nor sage
serpentinely influenced by illustrious examples or illustrations
of candor, it festered for peace and for the soul. Not sage
nor sybaritic, but sage and mercantile rammed like
the vessel against batlike rocks, it tumbled
from the height of rigor and of the dance, from the sol fa mi do
of another day: not sage and not sybaritic disguised
as a soldier gasping and hazarding among the pigpens
ransacking, in form and substance, sex had its way
with him.

●

Hanging faces, bronzes on the wall, brazen faces, saints hanging
on the wall of a solitary rented room, for four
days I wait. A poor room, weighed down by plastic
flowers, and lions at the door. A strumpet sea, and a
hick town, outside green doors behind the new
road, invisible mountains, the light's a diadem. Hills
then green horses, their gallop an imbroglio,
a stratagem for self-oblivion. It's still hot, and the sky
is stained with unmarked graves.

5 Poems for a Poetics

I)

Allow me chains of indulgence, save me from the sinking
ship, lofty thought drive off the argonauts from this
my dwelling of unknown dimensions; revive my lips imploring
alms, reduce to ash the remainder of my days
not so squared you can't judge justly, transparent
if you verify it, though anything but a tranquil exploration.
Where is one who comes, who leaves, incomprehensible I remain
and tramp up and down a peasant's night spots: thick
hands rasped breath crystallemums of indifference, I don't give a
damn!
hurled against your target. Pressing on shifty merchants
infringing on vicissitudes, no—I wanted to say, but couldn't hold it,
the
urine and the moon and commerce innocently crystallized themselves
to do me in—thus press on, sophisticated anguish of the
moons—thus make me understand! Night's routine (a lively night
was the night) routine of not finding not understanding not forgiving
the bagatelle that's my refrigerator, cudgels for the beast
so completely self-absorbed it begins sneezing.
Collision of beasts and of landslides, my dreams won't leave
me in peace press then the pursuit of pleasure,
I seek you alone.

2)

Practically wild I stretched out powerful rhinoceros on the
hillside of your capital: that is: I know not: I want not: you are not:
I see not: I stay not: not: not, not, not, capital of my
dexterities because I lost you peasant shouter of semantics
to the infinite, I'm not sure if I've made myself clear, but I no
                                        longer see you
taking shape between my stricken arms for the tithing of the score
that never took place. What I hoped to say flew out
the window and the softness of your glance fails to corrode
your gift of freshness: thought has nothing to do with it! I don't see
you, I've nothing to do with it: coalesced thought means nothing to
                                        me but
a coagulated collision of strokes upon the parochial head
of secrets. Secret of the night and of the tomb dangerous
adversary of the moonless, your miraculous parochial chiseling
ushers in my end and begins another one. Clarity desert
of the intellect runner in the mood for a sandwich, beside the
fountain sits the whore, crematorium of linguistics is the
farce of our credence of our credentials.

3)

For I tried to be clear. For I was dying by you, sleepless night owl
my emotions. For the nights dragging on like
a stroke I rhymed permanent luxurious lust. For the
roguish nights in the furrow of the nights I am truly without
end. For the insatiable limbs for the insensible beast
for the nights for the look, for the eye that at this juncture
hung itself from a vocabulary, quick recipe for ricotta you look at me
and don't see me you hear me and despair me. For the protagonist
who balanced weekly I reply to you: I have not, I see
not, I do not clear up the weekly reply that I'm so good.

4)

for I can't promise you that I'm so good. Trust me, there is,
for instance, in critique of things, a sign, upon my lips
that you are still.

Pick up your pen and learn to look around, risk the cough in the
vestibulary, nearly, a small circle even, dozens
what am I saying, hundreds of clear-eyed glances at my back,
night instead a rhyming without backup.

A clear night. Permanent light in the oval room. Soft
shouts, your thinking. Kaboom, so much for the light. Shouting
softly and gesticulating but without finding any answer
is fitting is proper for my rose feet. Particularized
sensibilities I don't aspire to give succor nor to be the one
aired by the first crops: that is: dedicated to the truth. What
a cruel world this is you exclaim but don't you see that I'm thinking
                                                                    seek

what you can, any kind of furrow, whore of the long
sly ears, believe me the battle is nothing but a semantic
rivolution.

Cropping up in his glance the reflex action of my harebrained
body the first crop. That is: pay attention: the points are three: wide
the shoulder thin the neck and the lips are soft.

Versatile blend of smells of certain small ambitions I can't say
are anything but evident everybody knows it. Believe me the boats
                                                                    in the

muddled rivers are rotund: I have nothing else to say, the
breath is a strategy to confound oneself in language, that
if you wish, and can, and remember, and clear is your suffering mind
with clear meningitis, the assembly rules in short discussions
returning to vocabulary, break my neck assume that I'm
like the rest of you, who in catatonic language mask the engagement
of your mother.

•

Lifting of weight and fate's peculiarities
little peeping doves my energies are taken
by your flying away like a
candy, liquefied vocation for
a semantic revision of our quarrels
our birds of a feather. None of the soldiers who truly
wanted to remarry knew how to tell me
who's the one who truly marched.

. . . solitary in the didactic realms
I held up, little brigand, disappointed by
such a miserable fate, oh
you see I burst and don't you dare run, the
miter over the piano dulls
sensations, the metro, camphor, red
and curved lips bricks of the safe.

•

The goatish sole-curving sky
almost vigorously promised: ignorance
and terracotta.

Believing briefly, beholding each other again, issuing
pentatonic disappointment laughter is always
bitter; soon you'll behold the rebirth of lustrous
plantations and the harvest, a temporary
blindfolding of fate.

Press your disengagement in the night
oversee your plans, *amour j'ai t'ai tué*: night
again the candies a blackboard I
slip through your misogynous fingers. Soon
you'll behold the chanting of fate, you rabbit
and I together in the evenings of death
reduced to an industrial love.

•

life is a vast experiment for some, too
void the earth the hole into its knees
piercing lances and persuaded anecdotes, I sow you
world clasped by the laurel. Though
too vast the mystery of your mournful eyes
though too false the plea upon my knees
I'd like impelled to tell you once again: sow
plants in my soul (a snare), for
no longer can I stir from kneeling down. Too
deep in the sun a dwindling life, too deep in the shade
the ball of wool unwinding to the hut, a sea
swollen by your eyelids.

"Lentement, et très tendrement, quoy que mesuré"
(Couperin: 14ème ordre, livre III)

1)

   Tyranny of relationships; absoluteness
of the extinguished fireplace gray and
monotonous is your undoing of my night
in the dead of night lunaria anoints the
true being, while desiring similarly to the battles
to disconcert. Before desiring the recount
of your ashen dreams, I extinguished
the oil lamp criticizing from the corner
this incandescent ill held within your arms'
white masonry and if the infallible
sonar of my meager thoughts
the indivisible defense of this filter believe
me: incomplete
the description of your malaise, the rest
is blood blue and vivacious: in the night of
my deposition when cluster by cluster
the grape disengaged itself from my believing
and charitable fingers it seems a dream
conveniently you sell your soul and the scale
yields.

When the heart's pangs soothe you
you seem a wreck and if you are one you
gladly sell the two hundred fingers that made you
believe I was desiring, in the night broken
by little sleepless dreams, it makes sense
this perfect uprising. But it seems
crack the boom yields, oval in the recalcitrant
catacombs and the heart, an erased blackboard
so much has the bull done. Unburden yourself
quickly so that it seems, a perilous blinding
still in your, undoing the pomegranate,
harmonious perspective: nail equal to the
flesh if you don't shoot yourself, when youth
with its violin struck up a landscape
similar to the new subdivided era
in the skyscraper of your soul I catch
the odor of a match, extinguished
no sooner struck and the sky, constant in its
cloudiness with open arms has satisfied
the needs of the flesh
(years) which itself seemed a flower when
they slaughtered the animals in the back of the
pestilent shop, just in case
in the hand yields, when the flesh swiftly
ring-around-the-rosy falls.

Response

contrast between wounds and the mechanism a dove soared
but I lost myself seeking stock doves. Right away I convened
actually I was about to drink, and this time the lemon split
into equal parts was growing in the tea-filled chamber pot.
Rough the pillow when you can't sleep, a rosette on the taut
garter, garter belt; bottleneck of difficulties. To be
in God's hands I joined my hands in prayer, fingertips relaxed by
an internal civic pressure.

Either a God or a shadow: for the would-be sleeper it was all the same.
Revoltment in the jungle of cobblestones or else clear waters
and fresh shadows: the feedment of our chickens is customary,
you don't laugh if they shoot at you. Wanting to go all out, I settled
on strict rations.

•

The sentinels beyond the bridges, sacro sanct
duties impose tripled considerations: if
you really are a crystal sky almost green
or else tenacity confounds the eels, tenacity
battling self-contradiction, yet another flight
of mine to the outskirts of the illusion that I might
conjoin with the azure rivieras, hardly
tenacity, here's what it is, not wanting you and having you
in vain, darkly discouraging surveillances
I receive you oh night in the crystalline hands that
joined me separate. Separation and the self-distillation,
of the herbs at the bottom of the jug a glimmer
of voices and the eternal beyond a song roughed out
with pride.

In the evening I didn't see any of the angels begging
my forgiveness, arms heavier than air, wrath
an impossible coordination of battles
when the mouth of the river bore us off.

•

Tender growths as dawn draws near tender growths
of this anxiety or anguish that can neither love itself nor
those who destroy me by making me exist. Most tender the
emasculated night when from muffled sobs of the crossing
of square with street I hear irreprehensible squeals,
the careless mirth of the young who still know
how to live if to fear is to die. Nothing can tear the youthful
eye from so much disturbance so many streets on empty, the
houses are undertows for untoward laughter. They taunt me
now that the shutters with a solemn gesture patch other fears
of even smaller men and if consoling myself that among
the living there is still believing, I conjure up your taut and sallow
face, with its hint of genius—it's to feel in everything
the crush of boredom of being disturbed for next to nothing.

·

Notarized papers for the inflamed a red
poppy ablaze as if it were your grotesque
hopes I'd say if it weren't that by doing so
I seek enlightenment of the projects despite
the obstacles inherent in your roughness. In the
stone on the street the instance of unblemished
objects if you misread them and in the girth
of the street a tandem as well. In the
modesty of enlightened subjects held sway
pools of meager blood earth covered with
undulating inkwells renaissance when
you are broken.

·

One foot on the ground, then you lift your foot, then set it
down and tardy the leg then the thigh and all in a
quiet tinny roar you lower it and in the
entwining your two legs touch ground. Then in the
ground there's tinned meat opening itself because I quickly
whisper I want you. Then when I set down my foot you chance
to catch sight of it floating quietly and the crystal shards
poke through like scarce or droopy mushrooms, in the black
wax. Then in the wax the uterus discharges and the uterus
is then that horse, cantankerous, he always gets his
way and then rides so gaily and then another tremor
until he's had his fill.

Then when it's over he heads out and shadows are on the ground,
           all a
loitering of empty forms ticing like flowers but
then unraveling and the intestines at rest beg
no, don't close.

Then in the leg the door shuts and the door clears away
the leftovers and the internal gurgling cries out cries out.
We'll go hungry yet another day, famine, the clock set
for migraines as we'll set off infamous, a promised
land and forgotten then your famine.

•

Fingers and brain refusing to obey, the order from on high, the
                                                    ambition
controlled by your body, a grudging separation of the ink
from your ambiguous hands. Gigantic dwarfs promising, glory
to the merchant, a tickling of the passions, mane trespassed
by a bracelet. Mane trespassed by passions
an equal enchantment for your arms, so heavy with
love.

Surprised on the street corner, uncertain I swooned
but pricked by modesty, I clenched my fists. If
you know it hurts you why did you do it.

Pricked by deception, a sterile deception, why
did you make it? that sweet? Sweet the arrival of tidings
steering you back on track in stead of the veterinarian.

Trespassed by the marching order, by the daring itself, if,
instead, it wanted to take me out of action to tempt me, again
if the demon overthrowing you doesn't disappoint.

Because everyone wrote. Spear that breaks a thud
your placid rivulet.

Spear that breaks a heart your thud.

·

Irony an even harder knee.

You think think think and it's the end. Of all your documents
enchantments. While you lie I sneak off, along the lines of the
mountain sonnet. Inkling inkling your gloves will never touch
a living thing.

The sonnet a barbarous thing. The headstone a match
that while staging the great instance instantaneously disclosed itself
a line of the future your hand and in your face, the
unhappy mob of the parvenu, innocence that remained in you
a pardon.

The mob a pardon.

The motorcycle a quarrel. The hallucination a lift

to the graveyard. Doubtless its most distinguished
representative.

(The only thing I care about
is not losing face
with its appearances.)

•

Relief upon relief, the white stripes the papers white
a relief, passage upon passage a brand-new bicycle
with bleach spraying the graveyard.

Relief upon relief with the white coat extending brownly
over the abyss, belief tattoos and telephones in a row, while
awaiting the honorable Rivulini I unbuttoned. House upon house

I telegraph, a spare bicycle please if the rest of you can find
a way to push. Relief upon relief you push transitive my
yellow bicycle, my smoking. Relief upon relief all

the papers scattered across floor and table, hinting slickly
that the future waits for me.

Let the future await me! Let it await me let the biblical future
await me in its scope, a twisted destiny I haven't found
making the rounds of the butcher shops.

•

Sweetness of a glance and a possible
lie to proliferate with hands
open to all visions, open because
I see you enriching the entire world
my small world of so many cover-ups.
And in the sweetest disinfecting of the
overflowing days, and in our truest
confiding that the road has ended
closed to each shaking of the door
I see you, exaggerating your stature
in my mind, your shortcomings
still unhoped for, to my still-
hopeful eyes.

Luminous the virtue of his mind
plainly translingering it awaits
the hour of absolute awakening, an entire
nation seconding my plans! But

on my mental plane it's not inherent
your bringing Babel to my
eyes that saw so much between two
devastated hills. I see the time, it's one o'clock
in my deadened mind, and you await
the hours that follow on the heels of death.
Death sure of its holdings nods
yes, come—as I dispel every lingering
and ceremoniously greet it. A poor creature
death if in the hell of the wee
hours it slumbers even in my arms.

•

Sweet chaos, a visionary sweetening
carries me weary into your picture garden
perfectly designed for liberty,
for lust and for all things that together
procure distention, from your ever-
shifting face.

From within this peaceful
little park I see you leaving, your
steps still slow, for another garden
and I know that like rain I will wait
until your figure has been resurrected whole
from the graveyard of my penumbras, my thoughts.

Like one deaf you seem to pause uncertainly
at the entrance, wire fence well-secured
against your possible departure, and
all around the gentle void seems
to be thinking of something other than your
return—seems, by expelling you, to infest you
with some punishment—I don't fall but am always
the one dying piece by piece. And
in this liquefaction of inclinations
the plane of the park tips over, the
wood-scent silences, and all about
still brims the modest joy of being
almost safe.

•

This garden that to my figurative
mind seems to want to open tiny new
horizons to my joy after last
night's storm, this garden is a bit
white and maybe green if I want to color it
and waits to be set foot in, charmless
its placidity. A dead corner
a life that descends without desiring the good
into cellars brimming with significance now
that death itself has announced with
its decanting its own importance. And in the
decanting a little dream insists on being
remembered—I am peace it almost screams
and you've forgotten my solemn shores!
But it's quiet the garden—paradise by a twist
of fate, it's naught what you seek
beyond I who am renunciation, it announces
to me, that firmament I sought

at first sorrowful then wary in its self-creating.

•

A whispering peace, I found you
engaged in making yourself scarce. It's
as if, in your void crowned with impudent
umbilici, a true history were born
truly faithful to your words.
And in the engagement I find necessary
to take up for your dwelling still
a flower shakes, it's my
mind sickened by so many false solutions.

Overturning stylistics, carrying off
that hubbub of shrewd cars
and returning promptly after supper
I glimpse, in fact, your still-undusted
kingdom, and still to come
the bandage on your knee!

to Braibanti

In your large smoky hands, there remains a goodness
that I don't feel, as a rival, in the shadow that
suicides you: meaning: let me not hear your desperate
cry or the giant imaginary coupling, that is your
guide. In your full suntanned lips I still see
a light becoming subtle comment and irony, more deft
your hand which speaks in turn, don't be silent. Oh
seeing the game of your destiny, I thank my destiny
with open hands, to meet you and still
meeting you, I find no nausea for my imperfect deliriums
I find no love under your true light, I find no more
perfect horizon than your hands.

But in the madhouse there were those who competed, even
for a dress, of clean, imaginary rags. Imagining
your lost cause, in my gut I felt withheld tears
that didn't well up for you. And then, all clean, I set myself
to write, these boring lines, so suicidal you were.

And suicidal I remained: imaginary, turned toward sadness like
an umbrella, which in its roundness parks my mind. I drew from it
a handkerchief, hemmed in blue, that soared aloft, meeting
up with destiny. Your destiny to speak softly always self-propelled
or compelling, newspaper illustration, imperturbable.
Your cause against the night was embroidered with intentionally
libelous arabesques. You slept, then you awoke, rebellious
as always, from a rebellion lucid but grotesque. And your
books so well washed in their paraffin, trembled
in your demented mind, illustrious desire for another
end: your sojourn among the great. You were delirious, and I

readied myself to correct, that vice, imperturbable
ending of your gargantuan day.

A gargantuan newspaper: with little indentations in its
print, inflections inflexible its manuscript. But
in the eternal reiterating of things, objects, and paraffins there was
also your presence, shifty, hawking papers. Stock-
still I looked at you, visceral, betraying public opinion.

Duties betraying me, imposed on me by chance, I shivered, maybe
you were master. An unbending reed, perchance, and seven
doors at the entrance of your magnificent castle.

Maybe you were magnificent, enflamed, by a real case, magnificent
in your bartering swallows for ants.

                            •

The heart ponders: nothing can stop it from pondering
"the heart is good," I'm fed up
with driving the rhinoceros. But if winning
war is honor, glimmering, virtue's
fine precision (yawning) then conquering the heart
is revenge!

to *S.*

So many people, and not all vain
in me or oleographic. Trembling on your
passageways, I plead for help or God, it's all the same
to my regurgitating senses, on the prow.
And right at the commencing, new
help extends, a window, ashen calls,
on filth to help it.

And I have only one complaint, that upon seeing
your vision, you do not call or gaily
flower about my perfumed body
of guileless indolence.

•

It's much easier for me to see your closed face
than happily impose upon myself closed rules. And deceiving
myself, or the others, I drill into the closed forms, and derive
from them a closed harmony, to your verbum, to your mysticism
unstoppable fist of dust.

Without lamenting over winter, which bombards your
eyebrows, I repudiate irony and stretch it out flat
till dawn derives from it: scientific laws, for
my growing vain annuity.

BAD POETRY for YOU

for Massimo Ferretti

With quick sure strokes: I bring you my celebration, my
celebrating vain glory, in a spell cast by merchants
and an industrious offspring. The giant bridges are dwarfs
when I come down from my blessed roof, and advance, a
most assured avant-garde—(more so among the plebes, a bit
mysterious to us).

But having found you—intent on polishing asphalts—I roll out
of my bed, climb to the roof, and beat you up. Or else
I stay up there, unsure whether to bless you or to possess you, in short
promiscuously melded with the sky, that goatish as
milk, promises nothing.

And it doesn't promise to cripple you: or to clone you, it asks
only for a rematch, and to disown you.

•

Maybe I'll die, maybe I'll leave you these
poor trifles as a memento: don't distribute
any thoughts in the woods for the poor, but
upon the rich, bestow all my blood.

And my blood in rich rivulets refuses
to be surprised: promiscuity with the neighbors
or a woof in the woods. Clasp about
me your flowered hand, depart for
yet another case of bloodless flowering, I
have never promised, permitted, my being
the one who pines away.

But on the trail of life there's a battle
of puppies, spectacular fan for
my condolences. Once more tie the cart
to my lips, which condescending to
speak, strangle, the blood and the vision
in an incest of smiles, promiscuity
sly blemishes. So many reasons for my
equivocal camouflage: a little womb
breathing, a voice falling silent, and the neglected
aspirin that remembers: death is a sweet
companion, retiring you from aspirations.

Dead I engage the traumatological line
to house these words: write them on
my lost grave: "this one can't write, she dies
roosting on the basket of undigested things
her manias uncertain."

•

Uncertain her expectations, and the flowers in
mourning, admonish. Bombarded by a river
of words, she argues, chooses a path, hardly
a match for her dexterities, were there any
to contribute to the great reformation of such tenacious
thoughts. She puts her right hand on the wheel
breaks it and deftly, embarks upon magnificent
rivers.

●

In purely human terms, as if his journey
had been cut short, I told him: "don't buttonhole
friendship," "it's definitive." If journeys bear
no fruit, if they are fruitless, at least take off your shirt
so I can see your sweat.

And he answered me: "if
a whole line is straight, clear, if the whole of my
belonging is straightforward," and I: "you're not the only one on the
straight snaking line, for it snakes back on itself, it kisses your
hand." And he replied: "but I head out in a huff, pointlessly
reflecting on your words."

"They emaciate me."—viaduct conducive to the madness
of knowing you with me, but distant, unreachable, like
the secret stabbing at the heart of things. They wither
becoming sparser, repeated endlessly, in tight garland
about your scanty brow.

I inherited the grass, things, the hammers on your
brow a tragedy turning ever grimmer.
I inherited from the grass its grim color, it cuts
the fodder in two. And it chisels, the future, before
you conform to yourself (before you saved yourself)
I fell. You fall trembling, subjugated, by your immense
brow.

And there was nothing other than fodder. Holed up I found
two of them, chiseled with the master's touch. Trembling, trembling
troubles, little shining plates.

•

"And then I'm not the type to be a rancorist" and
fleeing then she saw, ex-peasant that she was, one has
to square accounts. She flees, would like to cry, or at least
sit down for a bit, but "I'm not a rancorist" and she
keeps all the slaver in her mouth.

Strange this communion of thoughts, strange this
equal sniffing of each other, strange this sleeping pill not
pricking, overdoing it, deriving nothing from the lesson
but satisfaction. (And as she descended the stairs pricking

her eye were the words "I love you my dear
for settling everything.")

•

And with everything settled, she cried, a bit desperate
in her cell, biochemical her reaction. I'm afraid
I'm a little batty, she replied to the land-
lord—but what are you doing with the gun?

I'm pushing it into its hole.

And a shot fired transversally hitting
the retinal screen, then he sank softly onto the
couch, but was on the floor tiles red
and gray.

•

Beware the medusa: white slightly livid, the Giulietta
Alfa Romeo heads past you, quarrels the golden
silence and kindles in your faith a hope of
disappointment. Without paradise we were, castrated, in the unknown
faith in a tomorrow that doesn't want to appear vain but shoots
buds upon your sleeping-pill-addicted head.

Bird shit on the windshield drops softly
into the interruption of your dream. Liquefied you return
to your duties, one intention less.

•

Two tigers in the garden: of slightly blackened copper
of glass the living room, and your new science
clings to the horizon, may you feel
the need for it.

And then the sentinel fires and flees, leaving you
undesirable upon your couch. Then escape
comes to mind, finding another scale
to counteract the weight—of your entire length
pulling you by the hair. There's no solvent
that doesn't bicker: stretch out, reflect, and announce
sad dawns, bashful sciences, pornographic
photographs and even, in the hop of a bird
little true things. Issuing devices you
revive, stretched out with soft drinks—you overdo yourself,
that living room letting you die, in an ill-starred
glass that punishes you.

•

How beautiful these poppies are. They spiritualize
the grass, which grates cheeses from them.

Rio Claro: mechanized center: flowers (with
no names) extend a helping hand. It drizzles
and saddened (if you are) extend an arm to the
wind and the sparse rain.

Then you feel deferred: they've whisked away
all their breasts from the giantesses! Once again extend
a helping hand to the umbrella, and extend
a frugal foot to the earth, little sneezing monstrous
dust. Don't get caught without
an umbrella: it's raining like hell now that you've smelled
the full scent of the flowers (if there were any).

•

Complicity's arches by the sea, Easter
of the beautiful, arches of the cold in your
personal Noah's Ark: a frigid engloving
body and soul: for a foal, fingertip
ineffable affirmation of boredom,
distension of the glove in the hand and
thus a ball point useful in adjusting
true things.

Which would rather be sitting there
indolently bathing, stretching coats-of-arms
from your speech, they smooth it out and
then display it to the public.

What do they display? Your incongruities
then a smack on the behind then another
little thing: his heart identifying
with wine. Lesbian smack, or good-for-nothing
then another little sadness, your
scissors, snipping, each inclination
toward duty.

(transparent sleepless your wetting
the cat's head, its tail, when
its own heat drove it wild.)

•

I sell you my kitchen burners, then you scratch them
and sit unprepared on the desk
if I sell you the featherweight yoke of
my infirm mind, the lighter my load, the happier
I am. Undone by the rain
and by pangs incommensurable menstruation
senility drawing near, petrolific
imagination.

.

A cry in the mouth that not even
tranquilizers can relieve
completely isolated from its fellow
thermic filth, homely virtue
of sneezing, with an extra cast on the
foot, your hunger of crystalline relaxations
limps so badly, features
of a smaller universe, a show
of necessary feelings, small
semblance. From the dead the order to
depart, dozing in the last
farewell—taking in God's bounty with
frank ease.

We with a flat tire couldn't
bridge the distance with a yell
and were swept away, unnecessary plan
toward unattainable altitudes:
with this craving for caresses, which
shall never deflate your sails
but exposes the hinges of a poverty
that sniffing at its belongings
spoke of no longer being
able to walk.

Dialogue with Poets

From poet to poet: in sterile language, that
appropriates benediction and makes of it a little
game or gesture, slowing the pace over the river
to let every truth be told. From poet in poet:
like hawks, preying on the wind
that carries them, helping to ameliorate
hunger. Step upon step: a futile motive that
boosts their spirits, seeing their reputations grow, the literati
shirts open for a tan, under the sun
of all tranquilities: one slight miscalculation
and they're borne into the hereafter, death
descending, clutching them so tight.

Ironically fake, or is there a grain of truth? that I
can call yours also?

But in the river of possibilities there sprang up
also a little nocturnal star: my vanity, to be
among the vanguard a giant of passion: a Christ-emblem
of the renunciations. Announcing chastity, dilemmas
resolvable and not, knowing how to parry the emblem
from virile mouths, I learned you'd shot yourself
with a bullet in the head: self-dominion if
the hurricane roars in the night. Hurricane particle
of such a vast dominion it furrows even your brow
of unexistential shames.

And at the stroke, I saw you again, dead on the floor, displaying
nonsense, stretching your shirt to all four corners
spitting conformist kicks toward the earth.

•

Seeking an answer to an unconscious voice
or through it thinking to find one—I saw the muses
enchanting themselves, stretching empty veils on their hands
not correcting themselves before the portal. Seeking an answer
which would reveal, the orgiastic sense of these events
the particular darkening of a fate opposing
through brief bursts of light—the only sense
the splendid gesture: not forgetting, letting
the walls chafe the skin, notwithstanding estrangements
and not revolting, against this wrong crushing
and sobbing, which is my moon on my face
the scent of angels on my arms, my step firm and not
furtive: a slow but accomplished ruin:
and not turning away from lowly things, writing them all down
supine.

•

If you want, I don't know, if you can, relight the fuse
terribly cold (cotton wool in the sky
still a pearl) though saddened, raising to the sky
mud-filled hands.

Attempting a solution: even if it's only death
undivided from your ascending, sun.

•

To be able to rest in your heart, in your fire
of spent embers, freely renouncing
my freedom. Or to move you to pardon,
losing the hour, that triumphant craves
a hard heart, of flint, so menacing
it loses the cause, the origins
of ardor.

To be able to dance with the hours, gaily
anticipating sciences, without imprinting
your face upon a stone. To be able to mortar
with you the thousand stones, conjoined
in a ring, which are thin ivy
binding our eyes. To be able to castrate
the desires, their purities unraveling into the river
where the dancers of night-suicide
orgiastically drift past. To be able to announce
that desires aren't absurd, but
true song, a flea in the ear
act of love, or else the true word
rising in your heart.

•

Hope born free of disappointments
what unhoped-for joy is then
this crazed match of mine
in air that whinnies for oxygen
and taints unfathomable bonds?

Fortified by hope make the best
of things, in the field
of cocoa and low-hanging leaves.

Chocolate whinny you open
my veins to the smell of
painkillers rushing and
filling, my blood with
blue bubbles.

•

Inexplicable or exemplary
generous and trite you let yourself indulge
a few old habits.

Quivering tongue in one's mouth, a wing-beat
that is language.

One felt then the need to raise, pyramids to the
truth (or to setting it in motion).

•

Bloodied all over his overalls seem
incorrigible from a cultural perspective.

Raptus seated, at the Piccoli Angioli Bar, near the
Fountain of the Virgin, who today happens to be me.

Acknowledging his cowardice, he strikes the prize on the table,
and from countless realities, picks one.

.

Loving you and unable to stop loving you, inconvenience
I endured once and once only, only
to backslide. Enduring yourself you invited: speaking
more clearly, lacerating the air with obtuse little
shouts, then disinfecting the air itself, and
calling it love too, so much it parted you
from my arms consumed with envy, from my
secret tantrums, from your inclined face
which never blamed or only somewhat, my bustling
the mind's clocks around your body.

Loving despite dullness, contempt
born and dead, loving for the whole long road
leading to the field where you carefully saved
the yellow coins, which spoke of other quarrels
of other usuries, of other enchantments all of them
transplanted in a single being clinging to
a tree. And tenacious you invited: and tenacious
I warded you off; the dance of the embroidered hems
the stitchery so marvelous that it was not for
us to rumple it with our second-rate
caresses. It was not for us to
come to terms, it was not for you to decide if that woolen
yarn really led to that hut.

There is only shadow around the hut, only
dead mounts and voids around my secret
only you with your glance can foresee
this loneliness querying to return
again, dead upon the prey.

·

But you wouldn't return: you lay down half dead
in a field of wheat, waiting for the sky.
I took you home, I sowed you throughout
the olive groves, I pushed you into the ravine, and then,
seeing you were dead, I came to terms.

In the chamber there was the scent of incense, filtering
from the church silent mother who did not deny
that you might appear to me: squalid vision
in the scarce hours, vision and refrain, spurned
by your insidious hand.

In the chamber you were lying on the bed so narrow
as to be my mate, while you fared
anything but close, in a house of bordellos
closed only to me. You lived in the very air!
and it was a self-querying, this silence, that
dragged oblivion throughout its sentences. In the
small cramped house you appeared, impossible
visitor: to preordain my day, to
tell me to come to terms. I wish I'd left you
in the field! smiling you stretched your hand to the clouds
and then hurled yourself into the depths.

                         •

And dying for you is vain: but still more vain
this dissembling a semblance of vitality
when you ran me out of the village, twinned
your eyes.

Still more vain this wish to be for others
other than Christian; a guide in effect or
one guided, a stone or a thud, a mine
or its dust. Even vainer to fancy themselves bearers
of good tidings, of one of life's
triumphs, even vainer being, under extreme conditions
the expert sailor.

If life is lacking in courage: it's our belief
in ourselves, that robs us of it—courage can't
suffice, to ease the pain, to halt incurable
unsolvable diseases. (And I point my pen
toward a clear sky, that sails far-off
warily indifferent, lest you fall.)

Square clouds watch us and sigh:
one gaunts oneself, believing in rejuvenation
mumbling maledictions. Peace on earth
will be yours, if you ignore us, if you extract
from the miracle, mere semblance.

The dead bless the soul, and then cart it off
to the nearest graveyard.

•

I feel so lonely, and I love you so, the wind sinks
its teeth into the countryside, pamphlets flying
into my eyes, and each and every hailstone says:
"you're not one of us." The rest of us laugh
at the storm, you dupe the chickens with your
tears, acquired on the cheap, your invoking
the word love.

And I become the other one again, the older one, who
kept me company, as child and as adult,
that other one the old one, who knew how to savor
the mystery of your dark and yellow eyes,
changing with age, lakes at first, narrows
now.

Wanting to say: you moor me, the wind roars
in the storm a fish, changes colors, because
the sparse rain caresses it, in the scent-filled
air, cats spring forth, fur on
end, they know what you know.

And seeing him now, I wonder, how to
keep loving, knowing him foreign to your
every gesture, moored to his sweep, my own
lacking urgency, and you with the crust
of winter, that you bless, from afar.

Latin his eye, his sweep both glitter
with a broom I sweep away the debris, which was
that soul of mine I call love before
you undid it. You've beaten it back into its
den and it doesn't dare utter a word that's not
the mockery of its own virtues.

•

My head pounds, in the pensione, wash the
pangs (manias), so I can't love you anymore
for I'm locked in my unease, or disaster
that appears once a year, adumbrating
dreams of caresses.

A girl I was, and I dreamt of you, attending
dances shorn of desire. Now it's the flame
that like a tongue, unites, beyond many incinerated
mounts. You dance, monster of the bearlike
eye, and I trap you, in the faded
bed. You stamp your being, in rivulets of feigned
innocence.

And now I muster for you, in the dead woods, a
complicitous smile as well.

•

A feeble little voice: it's enough to crack open the shutter
of the tiny window, to change the world and
its semblances are all one with your
migraines. Enough to crack open, open, your
sleep measures itself against the sky, of which
remains a tragic likeness.

You open a wall: another appears, to take
your pulse. Brushing against the wall you can't, don't want
to save those few hours of the spirit for yourself, to constrain
these its mysterious cells. You're left to feel like
a leaning pine in the midst of new pines
straight course toward rotted piety.

•

You don't remember my golden beaches, if as I suspect
pernicious you lean over the balcony, without seeing
anything outside your mind, which has trouble writing
anything good. Otherwise with each gust of wind
you'd be there, at the hanging, enriched by your strata
of richest metaphors.

And then you see the blue sky, tinging itself to spite you
it too leaning over, assisting you, awaiting you
while you embroider with the muse, other little tricks
or shipwreck. And it's sweet shipwreck in this
sleep so possessed, and it's sweet not thinking
of else but the mania of seeing, touching, hearing
sniffing your undivided rest.

Then you touch your foot, bring it to the olfactory, you
take it in your hand and you move closer, at a sign on the segment
rising upon the rocks, which concealing the houses
make a stronghold, for your little town that diverts itself
almost innocently, you've raised the bull so long.

And you push it, your foot, toward an open door, and you give
your greetings to the ladies (you don't shake hands
with the male). And then you redescend, along empty squares
through no-man's-land, alleys widened by the
rain, which you don't see so dry is the sky
unescorted you still descend, by your side the hour
that's a mixture of fate and of your making from each
sob one more existence.

•

Light falls upon your head uncertainly, but
I see you all the same; believe in me
may I always see you the same way.

The light now no longer descends very clearly
upon your uncertain brow, its landscape
is all mine.

You have golden light in your elusive eyes
they cannot reverse your fate
beneficiated by my loquacious gaze the
morning when I met you, dancing, near
that bedside of yours.

Near that bedside of yours wept
the mother and it was I who watched you clamp
your eyelids shut.

By fits and starts you almost revive, with medicinal
herb in hand, I'd like to pay you back for
the pain I suffered at your bedside
dancing in the morning when I was sleepy
for your heavy eyelids that refuse
to raise themselves to the dance.

But you don't dance instead you lie stretched out
on the hospital cot where we met
it was a polite kissing of the hand.

•

At times your head assumes a guise
decidedly perverse: there's a new glint
in your eye that leads one to surmise new
facets of your illness.

I lay my hand on the air that separates us
as if I could touch all that unripeness: you don't
see it, you're too touched by your illness.

I don't withdraw my hand; I leave it there suspended
as if there were a void to disobey, and
often I see it transforming itself that soul
of yours you detest enlarging.

A stillborn gesture; it never changes that
head of yours done up with special glasses
as if it were cause for celebration your feeling
ill.

I step back, I no longer nurse the slightest
desire to enchant you; in your illness you're
a zebra moving, taut in its
preserve.

I lay my hand to the side, I see
specially the quickening of lights and lanterns
on your face; it's too late by now and you can't
aspire to the good.

•

Naked words on the tree trunk, naked
I sit above you, pure the intention, the exegesis
doesn't call for other exegetes. Enough that
it issues from your call, life doesn't expose itself
in corollaries without cause.

You have flames in your mouth and you're the moon
itself, you have an eye in your mouth to purify
this sob, that calls you, by the
letters of your name.

I've laid your name inside a heart
that wraps itself around a trunk, the
bark clings to you instead, and the
mountain doesn't cross you.

The impure gesture seems to touch on heedless ends;
your name rests coupled with nothingness
I lay you inscribed in the tough bark, and
you keep your vow.

•

Naïve houses, it's best that God remain
unknown, the taste of glass is like
plastic, no scent is as strong
as incense and the foot discomposes
into equal parts.

Dulled by tranquilizers writing, of
things unknown as is best, to venerate
secretly to penetrate. Penetrating
under the pretense of being exposed, one
raises that which lies low: cut
with ill.

And the ill discomposing into equal parts
wrote these octogenarian lines.

·

your motive not to scream, before the
cathedral; exile or chance don't forgive you,
the locomotive.

I'm quite unprodigal with kisses, you choose
in me a flayed rose. Without thorns
but the petals, in closing urge. My
motive not to dream, before unwitting
truth. My motive not to close, before

the settling of accounts.

You choose in me a motive undisclosed
before the rose unpaired.

•

Accustomed to dreams, to sleep, to sun
advancing shorn of glory, a clicking
of heels upon the flagstones.

Then enchanting with the same old farce
the scion of a living line
who scatters his greetings upon inferiors
living it up.

Who strews about with chaste
solicitude his command: don't
curse at the fair.

•

Spring, spring in spades
your twisting canals, your pine groves
dream of future flings, you're not
nearly as afraid as I am, of winter
when the wind shivers.

You snatch branches from the horticulturists, sow
hardship in my soul (that so lovely
stays upon its knees), you show me
that everything that has an end
has no end.

Or else you consider vanishing, sly one
hidden by a rain cloud
too heavy to be believed.

But my plaint, or rather a fatigue
that can't find its way back to shelter
deranges the leaves, that yesterday
I mistook for needs, likewise caresses
and which now scatter my ardor.

It's life I crave, decanting the praises of
even these beaches, or mountains, or streams
but I don't know how: you've killed your grain
in my throat.

You resemble me: who between one death
and the next breathes a sigh of relief
but it doesn't bother me: or does it? your
seeming agonized in the midst of laughter.

And people curse: are even fiercer
of you than of the space that consumes you
carrying you into my arms. And I
clasp a pale mummy that doesn't
smell at all: seeds issue from its
eyes, plaints, commas, remedies
and you don't carry the mountain into the house
and you can't fructify, these
sisters who keep vigil over you.

You seem in fact like a corpse in its housing
and there's nothing left for me to do but drive
nails into its face.

•

The field stands out clearly, and the
sky (trash-colored) reflowers
in the heights, permitting you
ennui, silences, and playful internal
laughter, while the sun digs in.

In the evening a keen wind starts up
rebellious by nature, but humbly
employed in sweeping my eyes
of fleas.

Evening awaiting that I be less
brave, that I still raise
my eyes to all this serenity which
not once has made the headlines
as dangerous virgin.

But in my closet I store good things
made friable by the sight of these
dormant mountains giving their all
to my memory of hunger.

I've also got a sadness in the knee
that unbends with every stroll
but infidel begs pardon and also
constancy. It sits and faints, haven't you
pulled up stakes yet? And purgatory

is not so rebellious that it doesn't attempt
to wear widow's weeds again in
order to find out it's not in vain
this loving, rashly.

•

In the evening the sky roams, a poor
thing it is through the window its gray
(though it was green) undulating. Or else

colors I never thought to reconquer
barked darkly at the windowsill. If
this dark virginity cannot

rid the heart of its psalms
then there's no peace for the one
who unstitches, night and day, trite things
from his lips.

It's not the house (stitched with tiles)
that guides you; it's the disintegrate
mystery of the ariel façade

that subtly promises you bliss.

•

You with all your heart are frightened
of air shaking you and losing you:
down along the illiterate façade
dreams are freed, large drops
of blood that you count
as they gush down upon the hands
withdrawn in the anguish of knowing
where the air is what it stirs why
it speaks, of such watered-down wrongs
as to appear, so many things rolled together
but not one forgets that dragging
of yours through boundless days
night and blood.

·

So many people, and not all are
in me bliss or surfaces, you comb
your hair while digging orbits from their
sky. Looming over your enchantment
the wolf of the she-weres, below
the house conceals its white splendor
obfuscated by prisons, those
gilded imaginative beaches
or else low-cut shrubs
while trees disappear in the darkness
the night in your distance
your dreaming ashen horrors, while
in the den the cubs awaken.

Descending from the sky a light as well
meaning I don't snap to it in the
belief that in the pitch black there are
lizards for your love.

The sky responds to such a chaste
intention of being enlarged
reveals its thumb or strikes it
in vain, earth lays down its pillow
on which you slept when I dreamt of you
selling lights to the teats that
await your arrival.

The night brings no reproaches
I stay out of it while I await you
you who cannot come into the stable
I start to understand.

(The moon counterfeits its own design
to enlarge you while you sleep and in vain
you wait for other bliss to be
within your reach.)

·

There is wind still and all efforts
fail to keep the clearing
firm in its resolve.

I hear the tinkling of the grass, it can-
not, love itself. Save by unleashing
fragrances into the air, disobeying
nature.

Rocks hatch snakes that right
this dawning idyll.

•

Face in the grass you smell what little
there is to smell. You're tired
want to sleep, but cannot. The
jagged rocks assume sardonic
poses.

Death is in the air. For now
it eludes you. When you return
to the pensione you kneel down.

Or would like to. But cannot.

•

Trailed by flies, believing I was
about to faint, I found you on the other
side of the mountain, whose incline
followed my inclinations, to
be the perfect citizen.

Flies trailing me, perfected the
mission to the good—I awoke, tormented
by tormenting doubts, whether to come or
to have, peace in justice.

Flies didn't appear to doubt
the state of my anxiety, and doubtful
they buttonholed.

Still trailed by flies, returning
home I saw the tiny window, leaning
from the row of empty houses. Peace then

in that little room! here an animal
can live quite well: I see ancestral
gods from the rooftop.

And the bands of the town, costumed in
red and blue instruct: there's a justice
gnarled like a branch, flies had believed

they could repent me.

•

Diana the huntress was wont to draw near
these woods, irremediably
lost to her, who in the hunt
sported with words.

If I move there's someone who slides a foot
in front of me and devises for me a trap
of images elemental. If I
stir the skyline also
undergoes mutation. Words plummet
down to the valley they remember
my three arches. The parallel
of my steadiness doesn't step aside
if I shout in the pass the rocks dig
orbits. Diana hunted: a heart

dug three orbits, one in the eye
the others withered upon my
lips. Words are puzzled

animals, they're a glut on the market
no sooner had I signed the check
than they flew away from me. Diana drew

the arrow; words fell, fly
through the valley. I move, catch
them again, wont to sport them in my eyelet
after the hunt.

•

Children own this town
there are no robberies only spells transformed
into urgent purchasing and selling, a bit
of wool for pungent feet, and a thick
mattress for the slope. There are only
women in widow's weeds, old lullabies
and the wish to be fellow citizens, like
the rest.

There are no widow's weeds in town at all
only turbaned women or other apishness
children playing with a harp, fingers tight
around a branch.

                        •

A sweating rock: I tried all the
steps; unsure whether to wash my hands of it
or to obey you, while you painted grim
punishing angels.

A cloud reaches you, makes of you a hidden
pasture, you're within, the sea
of flat plains, lingering smells, the
mist risen to the sky. And queen believe me
by now I'm painfully aware of
your indifference, when all the while
this sea of clouds reaches the summit.

Grim mist, nothing else around
but suffocated silence, by little lesions
in the heart that hides but doesn't pray, being
dead. They're cooking down below: food for
the workmen, those obedient ones, I myself
secretly savage, swallowing my own words
no sooner uttered. Mist or haze or
cloud, the lines of the future don't cross
this line—which is oil on the
wound, brink that releases you
and the silencing forever needs put aside
tidied for another life.

●

All the doors closed: but I see you, snatching
a fate for me; it's my dreaming that you open the
doors. Then I can't see you at all: I wake up
holding your good cause in my hands, a
chamoised flower struggles to be born. Instead death and
solipsism, enriched by your remembering me, errant
on the golden plain, it really is a
dream your saying that you're here with me.

Am I reborn? Do I graze on the grass? You instead remote
from every crude cause fail to appear and the ominous
forests are mine alone. Soul remembers and augments
body laments. Maybe you've given for my
life a vain propulsion. I'm so far from having you
better me in your hands.

•

You don't live among these plants that twine themselves
around this vaseless foot of mine, and
you can't muster in your line any song for
these my sterile lines now that you don't
draw your tightened lips to this
my shaded body.

You don't appear to clarify the mystery of
your non-presence, you don't incite the circlet
of flowers about my wrist, broken because
I can't hold you near me. Even the moon has
a merciful slope but you don't hook
tight threads to my hand which so far away
can't lift the weights from your head
broken by sobs.

I fear my presence wreaks havoc
upon our occasions, now that you don't revive
the horizon. I'm afraid of seeming strange, confused
in bleating this incomprehension. I'm afraid of laying
barren vines across your scarlet foot. I
receive no other sip from your parched lips but
this my impious mystery, the day's boredom
split into a thousand shards.

•

You weren't dead; you were only alive
to moisten my lips with supplicant
alms, to lay out frugal lies in the
Bergsonian manner upon my living crystalline
permissiveness, while you ate a horse's
horseradish. You weren't alive; you were only
dead, after so many ill-timed battles
in the soporific spirit.

I wasn't sleeping; I only searched for
clamorous unions between lost souls
who finding themselves in a tavern drowsed off
to the sound of the carillon—quite a dauntless
idea, but not a prophecy, not a
pardon, not a word, new, sweet
or merciful—just an engagement for
seas undone by boredom, just a race
for the pleasure of being sterile, just
a tavern for the evening's boozing, while
toying with the heart you spat large
fringes in my face.

•

Around this body of mine
held by a thousand shards, I
run crushing grapes, hissing
like the summer wind that
hides; around this
aged body that hides
itself I draw a veil of swamps over
plunging cliffs, settling
then, on terms.

Around this body of a
thousand swamps, around this
unsettled mine, around
this vase of unfulfilled
caresses, I never saw anything
but fish enlarging, becoming
other than themselves, other
than an uncontrollable anguish
of becoming, other than
themselves in the arcadia of a
literary world that fortifies itself
chasing cheeses; feeling
besieged, at vacuous dinners
by uncontrollable instincts
of predominance: ragged children
who stretched other limbs
clean as sleep, in vacuous
mines.

•

Notes rising abysmal from the fringes
of passions shrunk to the point
of seeming veracious. And then with a knife
I divide them and decant them, believing I'm
a fierce beast at the fair. And then with the other
side of the knife I finish off their edges
afraid that a new melody will issue forth
to irremediably compromise
my sleep.

And no new confusion is born of this
but an alternation of exaltations
depicting the hand scented with summer
again believing itself a fierce beast at the fair.

I don't remember which note awoke in
me that lament of hearing within many
voices, the pitiful ones, while singing
along with the ABC's I glimpsed soup pouring
from your eyes.

Music though does its part
and in the understanding of it dwells
my passion, that in its contortions
depicted itself equally frightened by the
mourning of its big eyes and its song.

·

Seeking in the last shreds of evening a hiding place
less suited than this one that stimulates my
reflexes in long obligatory naps. Or
finding in the tenderly streaked grass
an obligatory cruelty the day that
you fixed your eyes on the spring furrow
enchanting a world of beasts with glassy
tears that didn't fall but became embroiled
in your so rosy sleep.

Seeking in sleep which yields some ill-placed
comfort a frail shadow which was our
youth lost to hardships, when you would gild
the book of hours.

Afterword

Writing an afterword to a book instead of an introduction empha-
sizes a reader's "choice and right to a fresh first impression," as
Amelia Rosselli herself once pointed out in an essay. In presenting
the work of such an extraordinary and surprising poet, we felt this
"choice and right" essential to preserve.

Although well known in her lifetime, it is only recently that Ros-
selli, "poet of exploration" as she once described herself, has been
recognized as one of the major European poets of the twentieth
century. The daughter of Carlo Rosselli, an antifascist Italian phi-
losopher of Jewish descent, she was born in Paris in 1930. In 1937,
when Rosselli was only seven years old, her father and her uncle
were killed by the fascists. After the Nazis invaded France, her fam-
ily fled first to London (Rosselli's mother was English and, like her
father, an antifascist activist) and then to the Larchmont, New York,
where they lived for six years—a time she recalled with great fond-
ness as among the happiest in her life. At the end of the war, Rosselli
relocated to London before moving to Italy for the first time in 1948,
initially living in Florence before settling permanently in Rome. In
1996, she took her own life. The tragedy of her father's death (and
the loss of her mother when Rosselli was only nineteen) was central
in her autobiography, defining her and her writings in many different
ways: from her trilingual and cosmopolitan upbringing (although
she preferred the word "refugee"), to her political engagement—as
with many other Italian intellectuals of the postwar years, she was a
member of the PCI, the Italian Communist Party—and deep social
consciousness.

Discovered by the writer, poet, and filmmaker Pier Paolo Pasolini,
one of Italy's leading intellectuals of the time and her first critic, Ros-
selli published *Variazioni belliche* (War Variations) in 1964, the first of
her eight collections of poetry (one, *Sleep*, she wrote in English). In

1980, she published *Primi scritti* (First Writings), a collection of her early poems and short prose compositions written in Italian, French, and English, the result of her plurilingual experience. Even though Rosselli would eventually choose Italian over French and English—in the same way as she would opt for the Italian citizenship inherited from her father—her poetic language is a trilingual hotchpotch, a constant drift from one tongue to the next. As she declared in an interview: "Mine is a 'trilingual language' with which I had to fight in order to choose the language in which I wanted to write, and the country I wanted to live in, simultaneously."

Serie ospedaliera (Hospital Series) is Rosselli's second book and was published in Milan in 1969. Rosselli wrote much of it in the mid-1960s after being hospitalized for a mental illness she suffered from for most of her life, and whose pain shapes her language and difficult vision. Thus the title suggests a certain "resignation" compared to the "bellicosity" of her first collection. In both cases, the "variations" and the "series" insinuate her musical training (Rosselli was both an accomplished musicologist and a musician, having studied the violin, piano, and organ), which also inspires the metric structure of her poetry. In her remarkable essay "Metric Spaces," published as an appendix of *War Variations*, Rosselli, emulating the traditional Italian sonnet, gives shape to a highly innovative metric system, whose ground component is the word, any word—given that any word is a sound and as such they all hold the same value—and where the blockish stanzas suggest the geometric shape of a square. To this end, for *Hospital Series* Rosselli asked the publisher to use an IBM font, where each letter takes up the same space, as the font most appropriate for reproducing her verses' cohesiveness. On the cover of that first edition we see a series of squares one inside the other viewed from above as a reversed pyramid.

In sharp contrast with the consistency of the prosody and the graphic disposition is the explosive language of these poems, a furious cacophonic *crescendo* of semantic and syntactic accumulations where rhythm, intrepid *enjambements*, grammatical virtuosity, puns, audacious associations, and hammering anaphoric repetitions express the humor of an author who is having fun manipulating the language. However, underneath the blustery flow of words, there is a profound and raw realism that never loses track of the reader who is constantly in play, engaged in an intriguingly combative dialogue between an "I" and a "you": "If journeys bear /no fruit, if they are fruitless, at least take off your shirt /so I can see your sweat."

ROBERTA ANTOGNINI